About the Author

With 30+ years of ministry and business experience, Pastor James Greer brings practical preaching to everyday people. He excels in communicating the Bible with real life application. His love for God, his wife, family and church are unwavering. It is the foundation for the vision of Journey Church; to bring those far from God close to God one step at a time. His passionate, young at heart mentality is a draw for all ages. Pastor James is now semi-retired from his business, but busier than ever. In his free time Pastor James loves to take photos. You may find a few photos taken by him throughout this devotional book.

Acknowledgements

First, I would like to thank my wife Debbie for all her encouragement, patience, and belief in me. She's also good looking on the outside and beautiful on the inside.

Josh Poe, the Executive Pastor, for his encouragement and fantastic creative ability.

Sharon Jones, my secretary, for her encouragement, reading, correcting and then some!

Journey Church for accepting and loving me for who I am. I'm the most blessed pastor in the world.

PEACE

Acronym for Peace:
Planned
Encouragement
At
Christ
Expense

Peace was planned by the Father, purchased by the Son and provided by the Spirit.

John 14:27 NLT *I am leaving you with a gift—peace of mind and heart. And the peace I give is a gift the world cannot give. So don't be troubled or afraid.*

John 14:27 NKJV *Peace I leave with you, My peace I give to you; not as the world gives do I give to you. Let not your heart be troubled, neither let it be afraid.*

> **The kind of peace I'm praying you learn to have from this devotion is the kind NO ONE can take from you and only God can give to you.**

How to Use this Devotion

#1 Read the verse everyday when you have time, read it over and over and stay on the same verse all week.

#2 Practice memorizing the verse or one of the verses all week.

#3 Ask God to speak to you personally on how to apply it: what the verse means to you.

#4 Write your insights as God reveals them to you.

#5 Imagine you are in one chair and God is in the other chair. Talk to Him as if He is with you, because He is.

Ask God; Do you understand my situation today? YES! Is it too hard for you to handle? NO! I Confess by faith that You already have a plan for my good and I thank Him for it!

The Rewards

#1 God promises to bless you as you memorize and meditate on God's word. *Psalms 1:2-3, Joshua 1:8*

#2 God promises to help us have victory over sin if we will memorize and meditate on God's word. Psalms 119:11

#3 God teaches us that speaking the word helps move mountains, but you can't speak the word, if you don't know the word.

Memorization + Meditation = New Met Expectations!

WEEK 1

Peace with God

God wants us to have peace with Him. The peace God gives us, no one can take from us.

3 Steps to Peace that surpasses all understanding:

#1 Peace with God
#2 The Peace of God
#3 Peace with People

You have to have Peace with God before you can have the Peace of God.

2 Corinthians 5:18 CEV *God has done it all! He sent Christ to make peace between himself and us, and he has given us the work of making peace between himself and others.*

Romans 5:1 NKJV *Therefore, having been justified by faith, we have peace with God through our Lord Jesus Christ,*

Peace with God is a spiritual peace—it doesn't come from anything we do. It comes from what Jesus Christ did for us on the cross. You can't have personal peace that last without spiritual peace. God wants us to have this spritual peace and it can only come from Him.

When you read these two verses what is God saying to you?

WEEK 2

Peace of God

Colossians 3:15 NKJV *And let the peace of God rule in your hearts, to which also you were called in one body; and be thankful.*

Philippians 4:7 NKJV *And the peace of God, which surpasses all understanding, will guard your hearts and minds through Christ Jesus.*

Once we have Peace with God, then we can enjoy the Peace of God. This could be called emotional peace. God wants us to have a peace that surpasses all understanding that can only come after we get the Peace of God.

Are you allowing the peace of God to rule your heart? If not why not?

_____
_____
_____
_____
_____
_____
_____
_____

WEEK 3

Peace With People

Romans 12:18 TLB *Don't quarrel with anyone. Be at peace with everyone, just as much as possible.*

Romans 14:19 GW *So let's pursue those things which bring peace and which are good for each other.*

Matthew 5:9 NKJV *Blessed are the peacemakers, for they shall be called sons of God.*

If we want the blessings of God, we have to do the will of God. It's God's will for us to be peacemakers not trouble makers.

Who has God placed upon your heart that you need to do your part to make peace with?

You can't control what someone else does and how they respond, but as much as possible do your part to make peace with everyone.

WEEK 4

God is the Lord of Peace

2 Thessalonians 3:16 NKJV *Now may the Lord of peace Himself give you peace always in every way. The Lord be with you all.*

Romans 15:33 NKJV *Now the God of peace be with you all. Amen.*

God wants us to have peace and He is in total control of Peace. Know the Lord is with you and for you—He will give you His Peace.

Do you have peace right now? Do you need to ask the Lord of Peace to give you peace?

_____

_____

_____

_____

_____

_____

_____

_____

WEEK 5

Peace of Mind

Isaiah 26:3-4 NIV *You will keep in perfect peace him whose mind is steadfast, because he trusts in you. Trust in the LORD forever, for the LORD, the Lord Himself, is the Rock eternal.*

<u>Steadfast</u> – to lean, to rest, to support
<u>Mind</u> – frame of mind

The way we act or respond and the peace of mind we have is greatly determined by who we lean on for strength, peace, and patience. It takes deliberate adjustment to lean on the Lord for our strength and peace of mind.

Do you have areas in your mind right now that you don't have peace?

Would you be willing to lean on the Lord for rest and support in that area?

_____

_____

_____

_____

_____

_____

WEEK 6

Surpassing Peace

Philippians 4:4-7 _{NKJV} *Rejoice in the Lord always. Again I will say, rejoice! Let your gentleness be known to all men. The Lord is at hand. Be anxious for nothing, but in everything by prayer and supplication, with thanksgiving, let your requests be made known to God; and the peace of God, which surpasses all understanding, will guard your hearts and minds through Christ Jesus.*

The God of Peace wants us to have the Peace of God that surpasses understanding. We rejoice not because of our circumstances; we rejoice beause we have the Lord of all circumstances on our side.

Prayer gives the concern to God, thanking Him in advance with great expectation He hears and will answer us.

Lastly, we guard our hearts and minds by thinking on good things.

Where do you need peace today? Would you pray to the God of Peace now? Would you rejoice not because of your circumstances, but by faith you know the Lord is over all circumstances?

WEEK 7

The Gift of Peace

John 14:27 TLB *I am leaving you with a gift—peace of mind and heart! And the peace I give isn't fragile like the peace the world gives. So, don't be troubled or afraid.*

Real genuine Peace is a gift from God—not a result of our effort—a result of Jesus Christ living in and through our life.

John 16:33 NIV *I have told you these things, so that in me you may have peace. In this world you will have trouble. But take heart! I have overcome the world.*

John 16:33 MSG *I've told you all this so that trusting me, you will be unshakable and assured, deeply at peace. In this godless world you will continue to experience difficulties. But take heart! I've conquered the world.*

God has given us the gift of peace because in the world we will have troubles, tribulation, burdens, and difficulties, but He wants to remind us and us remind Him that He has overcome the world and can give us peace if we choose.

Is there areas in your life today that you are having troubles and need to remind yourself and God that He has overcome the world and can give you peace?

What area do you need peace the most today?

Gift of Peace   GOP   Pastor James Greer

_____

_____

_____

_____

_____

_____

_____

_____

_____

_____

WEEK 8

Remind God that He is Our Peace

Ephesians 2:14 NKJV *For He (Jesus) Himself is our peace, who has made both one, and has broken down the middle wall of separation,*

Romans 16:20 NKJV *And the God of peace will crush Satan under your feet shortly. The grace of our Lord Jesus Christ be with you. Amen.*

In troubled times we have to remind God that is what He said; "Jesus, You said You are my peace and I need that peace right now. God, Your Word says You are the 'God of Peace', please crush Satan under my feet today."

Today if you are struggling with peace, write these two verses down and tape them to the bottom of your shoes. Then, remember every time you step God is crushing Satan under your feet and ask Him to give you peace and He will.

_____
_____
_____
_____
_____
_____
_____
_____
_____
_____
_____

WEEK 9

The Power of Our Words

Galatians 5:19-21 CEV *People's desires make them give in to immoral ways, filthy thoughts, and shameful deeds. They worship idols, practice witchcraft, hate others, and are hard to get along with. People become jealous, angry, and selfish. They not only argue and cause trouble, but they are envious. They get drunk, carry on at wild parties, and do other evil things as well. I told you before, and I am telling you again: No one who does these things will share in the blessings of God's kingdom.*

Romans 14:17 NKJV *For the kingdom of God is not eating and drinking, but righteousness and peace and joy in the Holy Spirit.*

The real thief of peace is self-centeredness and pride, The only real answer to self-centeredness and pride is surrender and humility.

When our thought life is sinful, negative, and rebellious it leads to sinful, negative and rebellious behavior which robs our peace and joy.

What areas of your thought life are you allowing to rob your peace and joy? What behaviors are you allowing to rob your peace and joy?

Would you be willing to confess those sinful thoughts and behaviors and allow the Peace of God come in and give you a peace that surpasses all your understanding?

WEEK 10

How to Maintain Peace and Joy

Romans 14:17 NKJV *For the kingdom of God is not eating and drinking, but righteousness and peace and joy in the Holy Spirit.*

2 Corinthians 10:4-5 Webster's Bible *For the weapons of our warfare are not carnal, but mighty through God to the pulling down of strong holds; Casting down imaginations, and every high thing that exalteth itself against the knowledge of God, and bringing into captivity every thought to the obedience of Christ;*

God's Word says we can control our thought life or our thought life will control our behavior. If you want to maintain Peace and Joy, it can only come as a result of what you think on.

If you are not sure how to do this, use the "Never Again List" in the back of this book and claim God's Promises instead of focusing on your problem.

What thought life do you need to bring into captivity? What good thoughts and promises do you need to claim today?

Go to the back of the book and claim one promise today!

WEEK 11

The Law of Peace

Psalm 119:165 *AMP Great peace have they who love Your law; nothing shall offend them or make them stumble.*

Romans 5:1 *NKJV Therefore, having been justified by faith, we have peace with God through our Lord Jesus Christ.*

The first peace we all need is with God, without peace with God, no real peace is possible—the only way to have peace with God is to put your faith in our Lord Jesus Christ!

God wants us to have great peace with Him, ourselves, families, churches, brethrens, and even our enemies. To have this great peace we have to learn to love and apply God's Word (The Law).

Are you at peace with God because you have put your faith in our Lord Jesus Christ? What area do you need great peace in today? Would you be willing to apply God's Word in the area that you need great peace?

_____

_____

_____

_____

WEEK 12

Confusion to Peace

1 Corinthians 14:33 NKJV *For God is not the author of confusion but of peace, as in all the churches of the saints.*

2 Thessalonians 3:16 NKJV *Now may the Lord of peace Himself give you peace always in every way. The Lord be with you all.*

Do you have a strange peace going on in your life? It might be God trying to protect you from making the wrong decision about a matter before hand.

Do you have confusion or disunity in a relationship you are in? That did not come from God.

Are you trying to make a decision about a matter and are confused about what to do? Ask God of all peace to give you peace in the matter.

What area do you have confusion in? What relationship are you in that you feel confused in or about? Would you be willing to wait on the Lord to give you peace in that area?

_____

_____

_____

_____

WEEK 13

Peace or Panic

God wants to give us peace, but many times by our choices we choose panic.

Isaiah 57:19-21 NKJV *I create the fruit of the lips: Peace, peace to him who is far off and to him who is near," Says the LORD, "And I will heal him." But the wicked are like the troubled sea, when it cannot rest, whose waters cast up mire and dirt. "There is no peace," Says my God, "for the wicked."*

Proverbs 6:16 TLB *For there are six things the Lord hates—no, seven: Haughtiness (proud look), Lying, Murdering, Plotting evil, Eagerness to do wrong, A false witness, Sowing discord among brothers. (Gossip)*

Matthew 5:21-22 NKJV *You have heard that it was said to those of old, 'You shall not murder, and whoever murders will be in danger of the judgment.' But I say to you that whoever is angry with his brother without a cause shall be in danger of the judgment. And whoever says to his brother, 'Raca!' shall be in danger of the council. But whoever says, 'You fool!' shall be in danger of hell fire.*

You can't have peace and pride at the same time. Pride leads to immorality – proud, lying, murdering, plotting evil, eagerness to do wrong, false witness and gossip.

Are you allowing one of these sins to rob your peace? Which one do you struggle with the most? Ask God which sin you are allowing to steal your peace and confess it where you can enjoy God's gift of peace again. Do it right now.

WEEK 14

Inner Peace
How to Find it and Keep It

Phillippians 4:8-9 NIV *Finally, brothers, whatever is true, whatever is noble, whatever is right, whatever is pure, whatever is lovely, whatever is admirable--if anything is excellent or praiseworthy--think about such things. Whatever you have learned or received or heard from me, or seen in me--put it into practice. And the God of peace will be with you.*

We are a product of our thought life—our emotions flow from our thought life. What we allow to enter our mind is the most important decision we make.

Top Keys to Think On
- Is it true or a lie?
- Does this bring honor or dishonor?
- Is this right or wrong?
- Will this purify or contaminate?
- Will this renew or harden?

Are you allowing the right things in your mind bring you peace? Is there a lie you have been thinking on that you need to replace with a truth?

Allow the God of Peace be with you, "and the God of Peace will be with you."

_____

_____

Gift of Peace   GOP   *Pastor James Greer*

_____

_____

_____

_____

_____

_____

_____

_____

_____

WEEK 15

Strive for Peace
"Strive and you will Arrive"

1 Peter 3:10-11 TEV As the scripture says, "If you want to enjoy life and wish to see good times, you must keep from speaking evil and stop telling lies. You must turn away from evil and do good; you must strive for peace with all your heart.

1 Peter 3:10-11 AMP Let him turn away from wickedness and shun it, and let him do right. Let him search for peace (harmony; undisturbedness from fears, agitating passions, and moral conflicts) and seek it eagerly. [Do not merely desire peaceful relations with God, with your fellowmen, and with yourself, but pursue, go after them!]

Hebrews 12:14 TEV Try to be at peace with everyone, and try to live a holy life, because no one will see the Lord without it.

If you want to enjoy life, and see good times, stop speaking evil and stop telling lies. If you want peace pursue it with all peace.

Is there any area you need to pursue peace? What does pursuing peace mean to you?

Prayer: "God help me to not speak evil or lie today where I can enjoy life and see good times today! Thank You! In Jesus Name, Amen."

WEEK 16

Peace in this Place

Luke 11:21 NKJV *"When a strong man, fully armed, guards his own palace, his goods are in peace."*

When God is the strong man of the house it is protected. When God is the owner of all our goods, we can have peace about them. We are only managers of what we have, God is the owner.

James 1:17 NKJV *Every good gift and every perfect gift is from above, and comes down from the Father of lights, with whom there is no variation or shadow of turning.*

Do you have peace about what you own and where you live? If not why? What good and perfect gifts has God given you?

Prayer: *"Father in the Name of Jesus I want to thank you for every good and perfect gift you have given me. I want You to be the owner and protector of everything I have. In Jesus Name, Amen."*

WEEK 17

Peace by the Spirit

Galatians 5:22-23 NKJV But the fruit of the Spirit is love, joy, peace, longsuffering, kindness, goodness, faithfulness, gentleness, self-control. Against such there is no law.

Galatians 5:22-23 TEV But the Spirit produces love, joy, peace, patience, kindness, goodness, faithfulness, humility, and self-control. There is no law against such things as these.

These fruits are available to every spirit filled Christian. These fruits are the character of God, and the character He wants for us.

Examples of God's Characters

LOVE
1 John 4:8, NKJV He who does not love does not know God, for God is love.

JOY
Zephaniah 3:17 NKJV He will rejoice over you with gladness.

PEACE
Romans 15:33 NKJV "Now the God of Peace be with you all. Amen.

PATIENCE
Numbers 14:18 TEV I, the Lord, am not easily angered, and I show great love.

Out of love, joy, peace, and patience which do you need the most today? He wants you to enjoy each of these fruits.

Gift of Peace — GOP — *Pastor James Greer*

When we are lacking one of these fruits ask God to show us what sin to confess or what direction to go!

Do you have a sin you need to confess or is there a direction you need to go?

Prayer: *"God would you fill me with love, joy, peace, and patience today in Jesus Name, Amen."*

WEEK 18

Peace or Rebellion

Rebellion will rob our peace, power, and position with God!

Hebrews 3:15 NKJV *While it is said: "Today, if you will hear His voice, Do not harden your hearts as in the rebellion."*

1 Samuel 15:23 NKJV *For rebellion is as the sin of witchcraft, And stubbornness is as iniquity and idolatry. Because you have rejected the word of the LORD, He also has rejected you from being king.*

We cannot live with peace in our heart and rebellion in our actions. Rebellion caused King Saul to lose his peace and kingdom—also, losing the peace of God. You can't have the thing of God and go around the ways of God.

Exodus 18:23 NLT *If you follow this advice, and if God commands you to do so, then you will be able to endure the pressures, and all these people will go home in peace."*

Romans 13:5 NKJV *"Therefore you must be subject, not only because of wrath but, also for conscience' sake."*

Romans 13:1 NKJV *"Let every soul be subject to the governing authorities. For there is no authority except from God, and the authorities that exist are appointed by God."*

When we do what God commands us we have peace and those we are leading have peace.

Examples of rebellion that robs our peace:
- Young people rebel against parents or those in authority over them.

- Rebelling against governing authorities like police. *(Romans 13:1-5)*
- Rebelling against our spiritual authorities like our pastor. *(Hebrew 13:1)*
- Rebelling against our boss.

Are you rebelling against your parents, police, or pastor? Are you rebelling against your boss at work? Is there someone you need to ask forgiveness?

Prayer: *"God, help me to submit and obey those over me because I know all authorities come from You. In Jesus Name, Amen."*

WEEK 19

We Can't Buy Peace

1 Samuel 13:9-15 _{NKJV} *So Saul said, "Bring a burnt offering and peace offerings here to me." And he offered the burnt offering. And Samuel said to Saul, "You have done foolishly. You have not kept the commandment of the LORD your God, which He commanded you. For now the LORD would have established your kingdom over Israel forever. But now your kingdom shall not continue. The LORD has sought for Himself a man after His own heart, and the LORD has commanded him to be commander over His people, because you have not kept what the LORD commanded you."*

Saul lost his peace, power, and position. (Kingdom) Saul wanted to offer God a burnt offering that would bring him peace; but the only thing that will bring lasting peace is obeying God.

Have you tried to bargain for God's peace instead of trust God for the peace of His promise?

Is God asking you to do something like tithe, serve, invite someone to church, etc., but you have been afraid to do so? When we don't obey God's calling we lose our peace. Where do you need to obey instead of bargain with God

Prayer: *"God forgive me for trying to buy and bargain for peace, help me to obey and enjoy your peace today! In Jesus Name, Amen."*

P.S. Remember: Surrender is the Path to Peace.

WEEK 20

Preach Peace

Acts 10:36 NKJV *The word which God sent to the children of Israel, preaching peace through Jesus Christ--He is Lord of all.*

John 14:27 NKJV *Peace I leave with you, My peace I give to you; not as the world gives do I give to you. Let not your heart be troubled, neither let it be afraid.*

Lack of peace comes from lack of relationship with Jesus Christ. God wants us to have peace; proclaim—announce we can have peace through Jesus Christ.

One of the ways we evangelize is telling people about the peace they can have through Jesus Christ. Jesus wants to give us His peace so that we will be able to tell others about the peace they can have through Jesus Christ.

Enjoy the peace that Jesus wants you to have today!

Prayer: *"Lord, Help me to share your peace with someone today. In Jesus Name, Amen."*

WEEK 21

God of Peace Lives Within Me

1 Thessalonians 5:23 NKJV *Now may the God of peace Himself sanctify you completely; and may your whole spirit, soul, and body be preserved blameless at the coming of our Lord Jesus Christ.*

The real me is made of up of Three—and—the Power of Three lives in me. We are body, soul, and spirit.

God wants us to have emotional peace (soul), spiritual peace, and physical peace. The further away from sin (sanctify) we get the closer we get to God of Peace.

Where do you need peace today? Could there be a sin that is robbing you of that peace? Would you allow the God of Peace have His will and way in your life today? Spirit, Soul, and Body?

Prayer: *"God, please have your way in my Spirit, Soul, and Body today! In Jesus Name, Amen."*

WEEK 22

Peace & Comfort: Holy Peace

John 14:16-17 *TLB* *and I will ask the Father and he will give you another Comforter, and he will never leave you. He is the Holy Spirit, the Spirit who leads into all truth. The world at large cannot receive him, for it isn't looking for him and doesn't recognize him. But you do, for he lives with you now and some day shall be in you.*

John 14:16 *AMP* *And I will ask the Father, and He will give you another Comforter (Counselor, Helper, Intercessor, Advocate, Strengthener, and Standby), that He may remain with you forever.*

What we need most when we are hurting, fearful, discouraged, and confused is to be COMFORTED. When Jesus ascended back to heaven, He sent the Holy Spirit down to every Christian—when you get saved, the Holy Spirit comes and lives in you!

The Holy Spirit wants to comort you, help you, guide you, strengthen you, and lead you to the Truth! The Holy Spirit's comfort comes as we learn the Truth from God's Word about how to handle the situation and circumstances.

What area in your life do you need comfort and direction? Would you ask the Holy Spirit to direct you to God's Word for answers you need?

God's Word has a promise for your problem and the Holy Spirit wants to lead you to it and allow that promise to bring PEACE.

Prayer: *"God, I pray that the Holy Spirit would comfort and direct me today. In Jesus Name, Amen."*

_____

_____

_____

_____

WEEK 23

Truth Brings Peace

Galatians 5:22-23 <small>TEV</small> *But the Spirit produces love, joy, peace*

John 16;13-15 <small>NKJV</small> *However, when He, the Spirit of truth, has come, He will guide you into all truth; for He will not speak on His own authority, but whatever He hears He will speak; and He will tell you things to come. He will glorify Me, for He will take of what is Mine and declare it to you. All things that the Father has are Mine. Therefore I said that He will take of Mine and declare it to you.*

When the Holy Spirit guides us to Truth and we obey the Truth, the by-product is PEACE. Peace is a by-product of trusting Jesus. This Truth that the Holy Spirit gives you will always glorify Jesus.

Is there a Truth you need to apply to your problem? Have you been believing a lie? Are you allowing this Truth to bring glory to God not self or others?

Prayer: *"God please allow the Spirit to produce peace in my life today because I want to obey Your Word (Truth) and bring glory to you. In Jesus Name, Amen."*

WEEK 24

Prince of Peace

Isaiah 9:6 NKJV *For unto us a Child is born, Unto us a Son is given; And the government will be upon His shoulder. And His name will be called Wonderful, Counselor, Mighty God, Everlasting Father, Prince of Peace.*

Jesus is the Prince of Peace who longs to rule our heart. This peace in our heart is not dependent on our circumstance, it is dependent on our heart's contentment and condition. The Prince of Peace brings a state of harmony and tranquility—that can only come from the Prince of Peace Himself.

What do you need the Prince of Peace to do for you? If you don't have this harmony and inner tranquility ask God to show you why not.

WEEK 25

Equipping Peace

Hebrews 13:20-21 TLB *And now may the God of peace, who brought again from the dead our Lord Jesus, equip you with all you need for doing his will. May he who became the great Shepherd of the sheep by an everlasting agreement between God and you, signed with his blood, produce in you through the power of Christ all that is pleasing to him. To him be glory forever and ever. Amen.*

The answer to feeling inadequate and doubting your value is found in the death, burial, and resurrection of Jesus Christ. Jesus says He will equip us with all we need to do His will.

> **When we are doing His will, it brings God's peace upon our lives.**

Do you sometimes feel inadequate? If so, why and in what area? Do you feel you are doing God's will? If not why not? Have you been looking at your ability instead of God working through you?

Prayer: "God, help me to allow You to have Your will and way in my life and thank you for equipping me to do what You call me to do. In Jesus Name, Amen."

_____

_____

_____

_____

Gift of Peace   GOP   Pastor James Greer

WEEK 26

Don't Give Up

We're halfway there!

When we are half way finished two things happen:
1. We're excited to get this far!
2. We often become discouraged and want to give up!

Galatians 6:9-10 NKJV *And let us not grow weary while doing good, for in due season we shall reap if we do not lose heart. Therefore, as we have opportunity, let us do good to all, especially to those who are of the household of faith.*

Galatians 6:9-10 TLB *And let us not get tired of doing what is right, for after a while we will reap a harvest of blessing if we don't get discouraged and give up. That's why whenever we can we should always be kind to everyone, and especially to our Christian brothers.*

John 14:27 NKJV *Peace I leave with you, My peace I give to you; not as the world gives do I give to you. Let not your heart be troubled, neither let it be afraid.*

What are we to do when we come to this point in life? Look to the future outcome if you don't give up.

Most people give up right before the blessings come.

Things to remember:
- Peace was *planned* by the Father; It was *purchased* by the Son, and *peace* is provided by the Spirit.
- Peace: Planned Encouragement At Christ Expense
- Peace is a by product of trusting God's promises, purpose, and plan for our lives.

<u>3 Steps to peace that surpasses all understanding:</u>
#1 Peace with God (Through Jesus Christ)

#2 The Peace of God (Comes only after Peace with God—emotional assurance that God is in control!)

#3 Peace with people (Is there anyone you need to try and make things right with, you are not responsible for how they respond and what they do!)

Ephesians 3:20, NKJV *Now to Him who is able to do exceedingly abundantly above all that we ask or think, according to the power that works in us!*

P.S. This is my favorite verse, because I see it in action at Journey Church

WEEK 27

Blessed Peace

Numbers 6:24-26 NKJV *"The LORD bless you and keep you; The LORD make His face shine upon you, And be gracious to you; The LORD lift up His countenance upon you, And give you peace."*

We see blessings and peace come from the Lord. When we know that God is the one blessing us, keeping us (protecting us), showing kindness to us, and giving us peace it results in PEACE!

Do you feel blessed, protected, favored by God? If not why not?

Prayer: *"I pray God that You bless _____ and keep _____; That You make Your face shine upon _____, and be gracious to _____; The Lord lift up Your countenance upon _____, and give _____ peace. Amen*

You may want to put your name in the blanks one day, and your loved ones the next! *-JWG*

WEEK 28

Peace, Be Still

Mark 4:39 NKJV *Then He arose and rebuked the wind, and said to the sea, "Peace, be still!" And the wind ceased and there was a great calm.*

Jesus rebuked the winds and storms and they had to obey. Jesus is still in control of the storms in our life.

It's my prayer that you will allow Jesus to rebuke any storm in your life today. - JWG

Would you ask Jesus to rebuke the storm and worries in your life today?

Prayer: *"Jesus, based on Your Word the storms have to obey You, would You rebuke the storm in my life today! Thank You, Amen!"*

WEEK 29

Mature Peace

2 Corinthians 13:11 <small>NLT</small> *Dear brothers and sisters, I close my letter with these last words: Be joyful. Grow to maturity. Encourage each other. Live in harmony and peace. Then, the God of love and peace will be with you.*

This is written to Christians! God wants Christians to live in peace with God and each other. One of the keys to peace is *maturity*—as you grow in your spiritual maturity you will grow in peace. We grow in spiritual maturity when we read the Word, obey the Word and memorize the Word.

What area do you need to mature in? Anger, Patience, Joy, Peace, or Faith?

How can you mature in that area? Read about it, obey what God's Word says about it and memorize verses about it.

Prayer: *"God, help me to mature and enjoy more love and peace. In Jesus Name, Amen!"*

WEEK 30

Peace for the Entrusted

Haggai 2:8-9 NKJV *'The silver is Mine, and the gold is Mine,' says the LORD of hosts. The glory of this latter temple shall be greater than the former,' says the LORD of hosts. 'And in this place I will give peace,' says the LORD of hosts.*

Once we learn everything belongs to God—we are only managers—being good managers of what He has entrusted us to will bring us peace. God wants to bless our latter years more than our former years. When we are in the place God wants us, He (God) will give us a peace nothing or no one can take from us.

Prayer: *"Dear Jesus, help me to be a better manager of all You have given me to manage. Please bless my latter years even more than my former years and please guide me to the place you would have me and allow me to enjoy peace that no one can take from me! In Jesus Name. Amen!"*

WEEK 31

Gospel of Peace

Romans 10:15 NKJV *And how shall they preach unless they are sent? As it is written: "How beautiful are the feet of those who preach the gospel of peace, Who bring glad tidings of good things!*

I've never really thought of my feet as being beautiful, but if God's Word says so, they must be. I showed them up close to my wife and she sure did not think they were beautiful and did not want them that close. LOL – JWG

The truth is beautiful are those who bring the gospel of peace to those who don't have peace. God is telling us that part of our responsibility is to bring peace and good tidings to those in need. God wants you to have peace. God wants you to know the way to peace is through His Gospel, His Word, and His Promises. If you want lasting peace, you need to be in the Word and under the Word.

Prayer: *"God, I pray that your gospel and your glad tidings of good things will bring me peace today. If you still don't have peace, please find a Promise in God's Word that applies to your situation, meet the conditions of the promise and hold on until the provisions come! They will come! In Jesus Name, Amen."*

WEEK 32

Hold Your Peace

Exodus 14:14 KJV *The LORD shall fight for you, and ye shall hold your peace.*

How do we hold on to our peace?
First, we have to have the peace of God in our heart before we can hold on to it. If you have not invited the Prince of Peace, Jesus Christ into your heart, today would be a great day to do so.

To invite Jesus in your heart:
First, you have to admit you are a sinner and believe God loved you so much He sent His Son to die on the cross for you.

Simply pray this prayer, *"Dear Jesus, I know I'm sinner, would you forgive me of my sins and come into my heart, I believe Jesus died for my sins, rose on the third day, please be the Lord of my life."*

If you prayed this prayer for the first time, I encourage you to share it with your pastor or spiritual leader.

Once you have the God of peace living in you, many times what we have to do is simply stop trying to fight every battle ourselves and allow God to fight the battles for us.

WEEK 33

Give and Receive Peace

Matthew 10:13-14, NKJV *If the household is worthy, let your peace come upon it. But if it is not worthy, let your peace return to you. And whoever will not receive you nor hear your words, when you depart from that house or city, shake off the dust from your feet.*

We want to bring peace wherever we go when we can. There will be times we have done everything we know to do, but those we are desiring to have peace with just won't have it. What are we to do?

- Shake it off and keep going to those who want peace.
- Remember the peace we are talking about is relational peace not circumstantial peace.
- You can't control the cicumstance and you can't control what others do or how they respond, but you can control what you do and say.

Prayer: "Heavenly Father, help me to try and live in peace with as many people as possible, but when those I've tried don't want to live in peace with me, please allow Your peace to return to me. Please give me a double portion of Your peace. In Jesus Name, Amen!"

WEEK 34

Live Peaceably

Romans 12:17-18 NKJV *Repay no one evil for evil. Have regard for good things in the sight of all men. If it is possible, as much as depends on you, live peaceably with all men.*

You can't have peace and repay evil for evil. When others hurt us our natural response is to try and hurt them back, but God wants us to respond supernaturally by trying to live in peace with them.

God's Word makes it clear there will be some people that it is simply impossible to live at peace with. Our peace does not, depend upon their response it depends on our response. As much as it depends on us, we are to try and live peaceable with everyone, but when it's not if we have done our part right we can still have peace, because our peace comes from our supernatural response.

Prayer: "God, help me not to respond to evil and hurts with evil and hurts, instead help me to do the supernatural and try to live at peace with them in spite of what they have done or said. Thank you God, that even when there is those I can't live at peace with I can still have Your peace. In Jesus Name, Amen."

WEEK 35

Peace for Everyone

Romans 2:10 NKJV *But glory, honor, and peace to everyone who works what is good, to the Jew first and also to the Greek.*

Romans 2:10-11 CEV *But all who do right will be rewarded with glory, honor, and peace, whether they are Jews or Gentiles. God doesn't have any favorites!*

God wants everyone to have peace. Peace is a by-product of doing what's right. When we understand our purpose is to simply bring honor to God in any and all areas of our life, then we will have peace, purpose, and the power of God like never before.

Prayer: *"Father, would you help me to bring honor and glory to you in all that I do. Help me to enjoy the power, purpose, and peace You have for me! In Jesus Name, Amen!"*

WEEK 36

Don't Allow Your Mouth to Rob Your Peace

Romans 3:14-17 NKJV *"Whose mouth is full of cursing and bitterness." "Their feet are swift to shed blood; Destruction and misery are in their ways; And the way of peace they have not known."*

It does not say, "If you say a curse word you will not have peace", thank God, because at one time or another we have all said a curse word or two. God does not want our mouth full of cursing, we all know people that it seems that is all they know is curse words. This verse should remind us to feel sorry for them because the very thing they are looking for is peace they will not have.

Bitterness always hurts the one who is bitter more than the one they are bitter at; don't allow bitterness to rob your joy and peace. People that don't know Jesus is their way to having peace will try to cover up their lack of peace through curse words they speak and the bitterness they feel.

Prayer: *"Father, help us to watch the words we speak! Help us to speak words that bring peace not destruction. Help us to pray for those who lack peace and use curse words and bitterness to cover up their lack of peace. In Jesus Name, Amen."*

WEEK 37

Peace of Mind

Romans 8:6 NLT *So letting your sinful nature control your mind leads to death. But letting the Spirit control your mind leads to life and peace.*

What we think on greatly determines the actions we take. Wrong behavior is most often the result of wrong thinking. When we allow our mind to think on things like anger, criticism, jealousy, lustful pleasures, envy, and hatred we will not have peace.

But when we control our mind to think on love, joy, peace, patience, kindness, and goodness it will begin to produce peace. If you don't learn to control your mind, your mind will control you.

Prayer: "Father, please help me to think on the right things like being loving, kind, patient, etc., where I can experience Your peace. In Jesus Name, Amen."

WEEK 38

God's Hope Brings God's Peace

Romans 15:13 NKJV *Now may God of hope fill you with all joy and peace in believing, that you may abound in hope by the power of the Holy Spirit.*

The joy and peace God wants for us comes from understanding the meaning of godly hope. Godly hope is the confident expectation of a positive future in spite of our present circumstances.

What you believe greatly determines the joy and peace you have. Do you have the confidence that whatever you're going through will come out positive in the future because of the God of hope?

God not only wants you to have joy and peace He wants you to be filled with it.

Prayer: *"Father, I want to thank You for the joy and peace You give me. Help me to believe whatever I'm going through will turn out positive. In Jesus Name, Amen."*

WEEK 39

Peace Crushed Satan

Romans 16:20 *NKJV And the God of peace will crush Satan under your feet shortly. The grace of our Lord Jesus Christ be with you. Amen.*

Ephesians 2:14 *NKJV For He Himself (Jesus) is our peace, who has made both one, and has broken down the middle wall of separation*

When Satan tempted Adam and Eve and they sinned, the peace and harmony God wanted and created for us was lost. God sent Jesus to crush Satan and restore our peace.

What Satan stole Jesus restored. Because the God of peace crushed Satan, Satan can no longer steal our peace. Jesus defeated the power of Satan to rob our peace at the resurrection.

Prayer: *"Father, I thank You for crushing Satan through the resurrection of Jesus Christ! I thank You and claim that Jesus is my peace. In Jesus Name, Amen"*

> **By faith, what area in your life do you need to encourage yourself in the LORD?**

Gift of Peace — GOP — *Pastor James Greer*

WEEK 40

Grace Comes Before Peace

1 Corinthians 1:3 NKJV *Grace to you and peace from God our Father and the Lord Jesus Christ.*

Grace and peace come from God our Father! For God to become our Father, we have to have Jesus Christ as our Savior. We get Jesus Christ as our Savior not because of what we have done, but because the grace of God and what Jesus did for us.

We don't deserve God's grace, it is given to us as a gift when we believe that Jesus died for our sins and we ask Him to forgive us and come into our lives.

We cannot have peace without first having grace.

Ephesians 2:8 NKJV *For by grace you have been saved through faith, and that not of yourselves; it is the gift of God,*

Because grace and peace come from God, no one can take it from us. When Jesus is Lord of our life, we can enjoy the grace and peace that God the Father gives us.

Prayer: "Father, thank you for sending your Son to die on the cross and raised on the third day so we can enjoy the gift of grace and peace. In Jesus Name, Amen."

WEEK 41

Peace in Leaving

1 Corinthians 7:15-16 _TLB But if the husband or wife who isn't a Christian is eager to leave, it is permitted. In such cases the Christian husband or wife should not insist that the other stay, for God wants his children to live in peace and harmony. For, after all, there is no assurance to you wives that your husbands will be converted if they stay; and the same may be said to you husbands concerning your wives._

The Christian should not be the one eager to leave. You should never marry a non-practicing Christian, however, if you were both lost and one got saved and then the unsaved person wants to leave because you are a Christian, God says you still can have peace and harmony.

The closer a husband and wife are to Jesus the more peace and harmony they have.

Prayer: "God, I thank You that You want Your children to live in peace and harmony! Give me the wisdom I need in my marriage or relationships to have the peace and harmony You want for us. In Jesus Name, Amen."

WEEK 42

One Mind Brings Peace

2 Corinthians 13:11 NKJV *Finally, brethren, farewell. Become complete. Be of good comfort, be of one mind, live in peace; and the God of love and peace will be with you.*

When we have the mind of God in a matter, that's really all that matters. Many times, the real reason we don't have peace is because we want our way or the highway. If we want to have peace with God and peace with others, we have to come to the point we are willing to have God's way and will in the matter.

Ways we know God's will in the matter:

- Ask the question, do I have peace in the matter? If you don't have peace in the matter it might not be God's will in the matter.

- It will always line up with God's Word—God's will in the matter will never go against God's Word in the matter.

- The more of God's Word you know, the more of God's will you will know.

- When you're not sure, wait or ask someone with godly wisdom.

Prayer: "Father, thank You that You want us to live in peace and that You are the God of love. When I need to make a decision help me to have peace in the matter and that it always lines up with Your Word. In Jesus Name, Amen."

WEEK 43

Unity Brings Peace

Ephesians 4:3 NKJV *endeavoring to keep the unity of the Spirit in the bond of peace.*

Three Steps to having unity of the Spirit:
1. Have Jesus as Savior and Lord.
2. Have the same godly goals.
3. Deal with problems biblically and quickly.

Psalm 133:1 Behold, how good and how pleasant it is for brethren to dwell together in unity!

Prayer: "Father, I want to have unity of the Spirit with You and my loved ones. Please give me the insights and wisdom I need to have unity of the Spirit that results in peace. In Jesus Name, Amen."

WEEK 44

Being Prepared Brings Peace

Ephesians 6:15 NKJV *and having shod your feet with the preparation of the gospel of peace;*

Understanding how you are going to fight against the enemy helps bring both victory and peace. The only real power Satan has over us is for us to believe His lies. The more of God's Word we know, the more prepared we will be when the enemy attacks.

Every time Satan would tempt Jesus – Jesus was prepared to quote scripture back to Satan. One of the best tools I have is what I call the "Never Again" list. When I'm tempted in some area, I look at the list and quote God's Word out loud when possible.

NOTE: The "Never Again" List is in the back of this book.

Prayer: *"Father, help me to be better prepared for Satan's attacks and use Your Word to bring peace in the midst of trials. In Jesus Name, Amen."*

WEEK 45

Blood of Peace

Colossians 1:20 _{NKJV} *and by Him to reconcile all things to Himself, by Him, whether things on earth or things in heaven, having made peace through the blood of His cross.*

Colossians 1:20 _{TEV} *Through the Son, then, God decided to bring the whole universe back to himself. God made peace through his Son's blood on the cross and so brought back to himself all things, both on earth and in heaven.*

The only way we can have peace is through God's Son, Jesus Christ and the only way we can lose that peace is if we have sin that's not under the blood of Jesus Christ. Jesus paid the price for our peace. Jesus' blood covers our sins where we can have peace with God and the peace of God.

When God looks down from heaven (and we have put our sins under the blood of Jesus Christ by asking Him to forgive us)—God does not see us as sinners but as SAINTS.

I love it you can just call me *Saint James*, but the truth is, you could put your name where mine is because you really are a Saint and loved by God.

Prayer: *"Father, I thank You for allowing Jesus' blood to cover my sins and bring peace with You and to me. In Jesus Name, Amen."*

WEEK 46

Fake Peace

1 Thessalonians 5:3 _{NKJV} *For when they say, "Peace and safety!" then sudden destruction comes upon them, as labor pains upon a pregnant woman. And they shall not escape.*

If you try and find your peace and safety in the world, it will lead to destruction. Before Jesus returns many will be saying, "Peace and Safety" here on earth, but the only lasting peace and safety is in Jesus Christ here on earth and later in heaven.

The closer Jesus' return gets the more we will need the peace that can only come from God. Don't allow the Fake Peace to keep you from the only real and lasting peace.

Fake Peace is believing anything or anybody can bring you peace apart from God.

Prayer: *"Father, I thank You that Your peace cannot be taken from me, help me to become aware when I'm starting to put my faith in Fake Peace. In Jesus Name, Amen."*

_____

_____

_____

_____

Gift of Peace   GOP   Pastor James Greer

WEEK 47

"Peace of Respect"

1 Thessalonians 5:12-13 *TEV* *We beg you, our friends, to pay proper respect to those who work among you, who guide and instruct you in the Christian life. Treat them with the greatest respect and love because of the work they do. Be at peace among yourselves.*

God wants us to show the proper respect to those over us. God is a God of order and respect. One of the greatest problems in America today is lack of respect for authority. If you learn to respect the position (even when there's time you may not respect the person) you will begin to enjoy peace with God and peace with those over you.

How can we show respect that brings peace with God and those over us?

- Show gratitude.
- Do what you say and do what your asked.
- Don't be judgmental.
- Be polite.

Prayer: "Father, help me to show respect to those over me and those who are teaching and leading me as a way of showing You respect. In Jesus Name, Amen."

WEEK 48

Complete Peace

1 Thessalonians 5:23 NKJV *Now may the God of peace Himself sanctify you completely; and may your whole spirit, soul, and body be preserved blameless at the coming of our Lord Jesus Christ.*

The God of peace wants us to have complete peace. God wants our spirit, soul (emotions), and body to be at peace. God wants to minister to the whole person.

One of the words for peace is Shalom, which basically means wholeness and well-being. God wants us to have peace in all areas of our life.

What areas of your life do you need peace in right now? Would you be willing to set that part of your life apart to be used by God?

When we give that part of our life to God—God then begins to clean it and make it whole.

Prayer: *"Father, I want complete wholeness and well-being! Thank You that You can give it to me. In Jesus Name, Amen."*

WEEK 49

Peace Always and Everywhere

2 Thessalonians 3:16 NKJV Now may the Lord of peace Himself give you peace always in every way. The Lord be with you all.

I love this verse. The Lord of peace Himself not only wants to give us peace, but He wants us to have it always and everywhere we go. As we understand that the Lord is with us and for us, we will have peace always and everywhere we go. It's being aware of God's presence in our life and understanding He is the one in control that brings peace in every area of our life.

Is there an area of your life that God is not the Lord over? If so, today would be a great day to give that area to Him and enjoy the peace God has for you!

Prayer: "Father, I thank You that You can give me peace always and everywhere I go. Help me to enjoy that peace by believing and obeying your Word. In Jesus Name, Amen."

WEEK 50

The Tenth Part of Peace

Hebrews 7:2 _{NKJV} to whom also Abraham gave a tenth part of all, first being translated "king of righteousness," and then also king of Salem, meaning "king of peace"

Abraham gave a tenth to the King of Kings because he knew everything belonged to the Lord. Obeying God and giving the first tenth or tithes brings peace, protection, and provision.

Malachi 3:10-11 _{NKJV} Bring all the tithes into the storehouse, That there may be food in My house, And try Me now in this," Says the LORD of hosts, "If I will not open for you the windows of heaven And pour out for you such blessing That there will not be room enough to receive it. And I will rebuke the devourer for your sakes, So that he will not destroy the fruit of your ground, Nor shall the vine fail to bear fruit for you in the field," Says the LORD of hosts;

Learn to enjoy the peace that comes from giving the tithe into the storehouse (Church) and watch God bless you in a new and exciting way. Give as you are giving to the King of Peace, because He is the King of Peace. You can't rob God and have peace.

Prayer: "Father, Help me to learn to enjoy giving the first 10th of my income to You. Thank You for the peace it brings. In Jesus Name, Amen."

_____

_____

_____

WEEK 51

Pursue Peace

Hebrews 12:14, NKJV *Pursue peace with all people, and holiness, without which no one will see the Lord:*

Matthew 5:9 NKJV *Blessed are the peacemakers, for they shall be called sons of God.*

As we pursue peace with all people, God pursues us to give us peace. When we learn to pursue peace, we begin to see the Lord. We begin to see the power and presence of God in our situation and circumstance which results in peace. When we pursue peace, we become peacemakers –others will see God working in our life.

Remember, God's peace is relational not circumstantial, so when we pursue peace with all people, we begin to come into God's presence and enjoy the relational peace that no one can take from us.

Prayer: *"Father, help me to pursue peace and give me the wisdom to become a peacemaker. As I pursue peace and become a peacemaker thank You for the relational peace You give me. In Jesus Name, Amen."*

WEEK 52

Speak the Blessings of Peace

Numbers 6:22-26 _{NKJV} *And the LORD spoke to Moses, saying: "Speak to Aaron and his sons, saying, 'This is the way you shall bless the children of Israel. (Children of Journey Church) Say to them: "The LORD bless you and keep you; The LORD make His face shine upon you, And be gracious to you; The LORD lift up His countenance upon you, And give you peace." '*

Pastor James' Prayer:
God, it is my prayer that I can speak the blessings and peace to all who are reading this right now. Lord, please bless Journey Church and all those reading this book. Lord, please keep those safe and protected. Lord, please make Your face shine upon everyone at Journey Church and reading this book. Lord, please be gracious and give Your peace to everyone at Journey Church and those reading this book.

Personally, I want to thank you for going through this Journey of Peace with me! It's my prayer that you will have a peace that will surpass all your understanding, and you will understand because of what Jesus did, you can have peace anywhere and everywhere you go.

P.S. You might want to personalize this prayer for your family.

God Bless and may the God of Peace be with you today and always!

- Pastor James

My "Never Again" List

1. Never again will I confess that "I can't" for "I can do all things through Christ which strengthens me." *(Philippians 4:13)*

2. Never again will I confess fear for "God hath not given me the spirit of fear but of power, and of love, and of a sound mind." *(2 Timothy 1:7)*

3. Never again will I confess doubt or lack of faith for "God hath given to every man the measure of faith." *(Romans 12:3)* and "this is the victory that overcometh the world even our faith." *(1 John 5:4)*

4. Never again will I confess weakness for "The Lord is the strength of my life." *(Psalms 27:1)* and "the people that know their God shall be strong." *(Daniel 11:32)*

5. Never again will I confess supremacy of Satan over my life for "Greater is He that is within me than he that is in the world." *(1 John 4:4)*; "and He hath raised us up together and made us sit together in heavenly places in Christ Jesus." *(Ephesians 2:6)*; "Far above all principality and power and might and dominion and every name in that which is to come." *(Ephesians 1:21)*; "That is the ages to come He might show the exceeding riches of His grace and His kindness toward us through Christ." *(Ephesians 2:7)*; "That we might know what is the exceeding greatness of His power to us who believe according to the working of His mighty power, which He wrought in Christ when He raised Him from the dead and set Him at His own right hand in the heavenly places." *(Ephesians 1:19-20)*

6. Never again will I confess defeat "For God always causeth me to triumph in Christ Jesus." *(2 Corinthians 2:14)* and "we are more than conquerors through Him that loved us." *(Romans 8:37)*

7. Never again will I confess sickness for "With His stripes I am healed." *(Isaiah 53:5)* and "Jesus Himself too my infirmities and bare my sicknesses." *(Matthew 8:17)*

8. Never again will I confess worries and frustrations, "For I am casting all my cares on Him who careth for me." *(1 Peter 5:7)*; "I will be careful for nothing but in everything by prayer and supplication with thanksgiving let my requests be made known unto God and the peace of God that passeth all understanding is keeping my heart and mind through Christ Jesus." *(Philippians 4:6-7)* In Christ I am free.

9. Never again will I confess lack for "My God shall supply all my needs according to His riches in glory by Christ Jesus." *(Philippians 4:19)*

10. Never again will I be utterly defeated by Satan in any area for "The steps of a good man are ordered by the Lord and He delighteth in His way. Though He falls he shall not be utterly cast down for the Lord upholdeth him with His hand." *(Psalm 37:23-24)* and "Jesus gave the power over all the power of the enemy and nothing shall by any means hurt me." *(Luke 10:17)*; "Sin shall have no dominion over me." *(Romans 6:14)* for I am "Yielding myself unto God as one that is alive from the dead and my members as instruments of righteousness unto God." *(Romans 5:12)*

11. Never again will I confess that anything is too hard or impossible for the Lord for "There is nothing too hard for the Lord." *(Jeremiah 32:17)* and "With God nothing shall be impossible." *(Luke 1:37)*

> **"FOR THIS PURPOSE THE SON OF GOD WAS MANIFESTED THAT HE MIGHT DESTROY THE WORK OF THE DEVIL."**
> **1 JOHN 3:8**